# DOWNTON TABBY

CHARLIE ELLIS

## WHAT YOUR CAT REALLY THINKS WHILE YOU WATCH TV

Skyhorse Publishing

Skyhorse Publishing books may be purchased in bulk at special discounts for sales promotion, corporate gifts, fund-raising, or educational purposes. Special editions can also be created to specifications. For details, contact the Special Sales Department, Skyhorse Publishing, 307 West 36th Street, 11th Floor, New York, NY 10018 or info@skyhorsepublishing.com.

Skyhorse® and Skyhorse Publishing® are registered trademarks of Skyhorse Publishing, Inc.®, a Delaware corporation.

Visit our website at www.skyhorsepublishing.com.

10 9 8 7 6 5 4 3 2 1

Library of Congress Cataloging-in-Publication Data is available on file.

Cover design by Michael Short
Images © Shutterstock

Print ISBN: 978-1-5107-3314-5
E-Book ISBN: 978-1-5107-3317-6

Printed in China

You probably think that your cat pays no attention to the shows you watch; you may even kid yourself that Tiddles and Snowball spend time in the living room because they want to be with you. However, you couldn't be more wrong: cats are television addicts and there's no denying it. Our team of dedicated researchers have been studying the nation's felines, and we can finally reveal what goes through their meowing minds when they're glued to the tube.

Prepare to be enlightened! And don't even THINK about changing the channel until your four-legged friend has finished watching . . . .

AVOID! AVOID ALL OF THEM! I REPEAT: DON'T KISS, DON'T MARRY, JUST PLAIN AVOID.

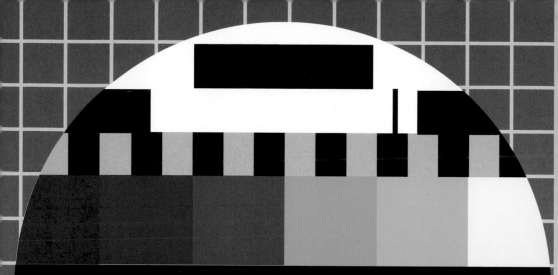

COME ON, LADS!
YOU CAN CLAW ONE BACK!

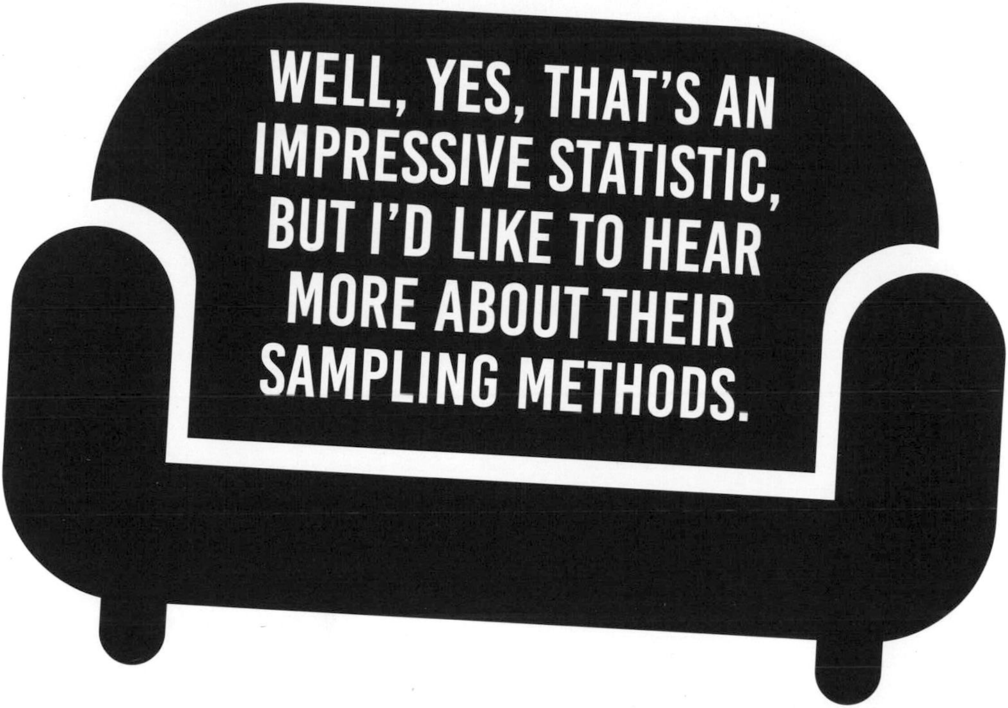
WELL, YES, THAT'S AN
IMPRESSIVE STATISTIC,
BUT I'D LIKE TO HEAR
MORE ABOUT THEIR
SAMPLING METHODS.

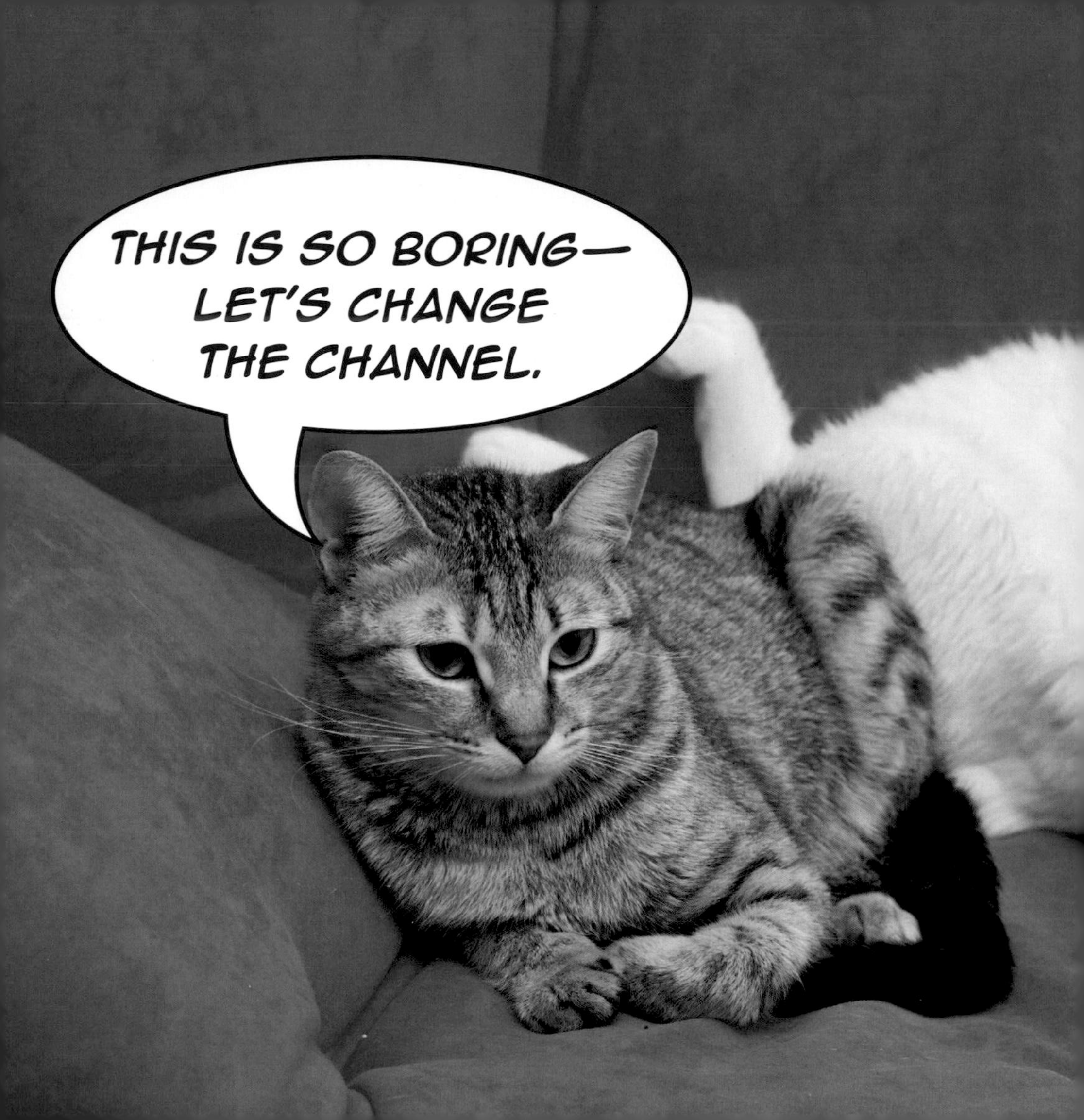
THIS IS SO BORING—LET'S CHANGE THE CHANNEL.

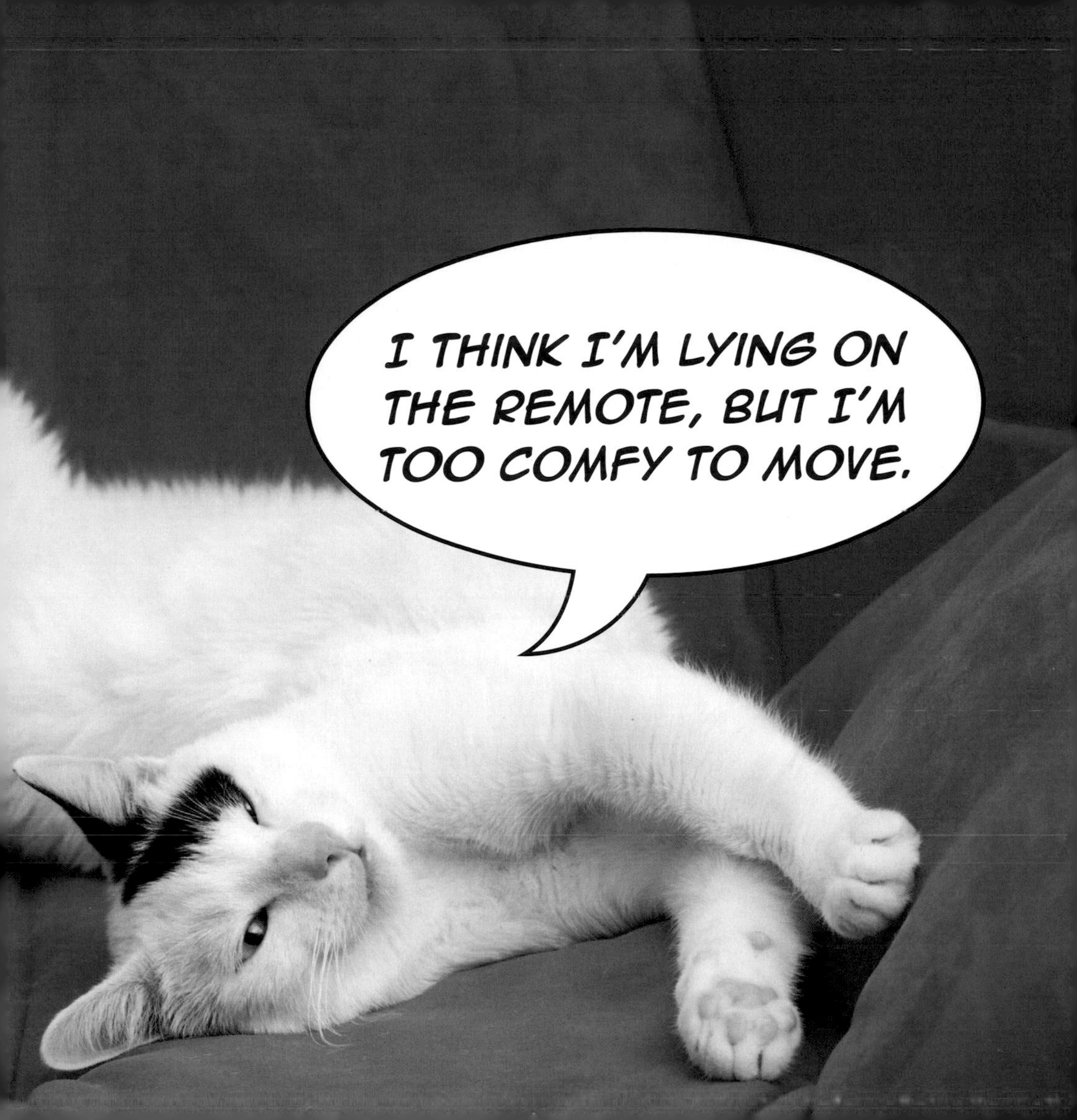
I THINK I'M LYING ON THE REMOTE, BUT I'M TOO COMFY TO MOVE.

HURRY UP, KEVIN—
*GAME OF THRONES*
IS ABOUT TO START!

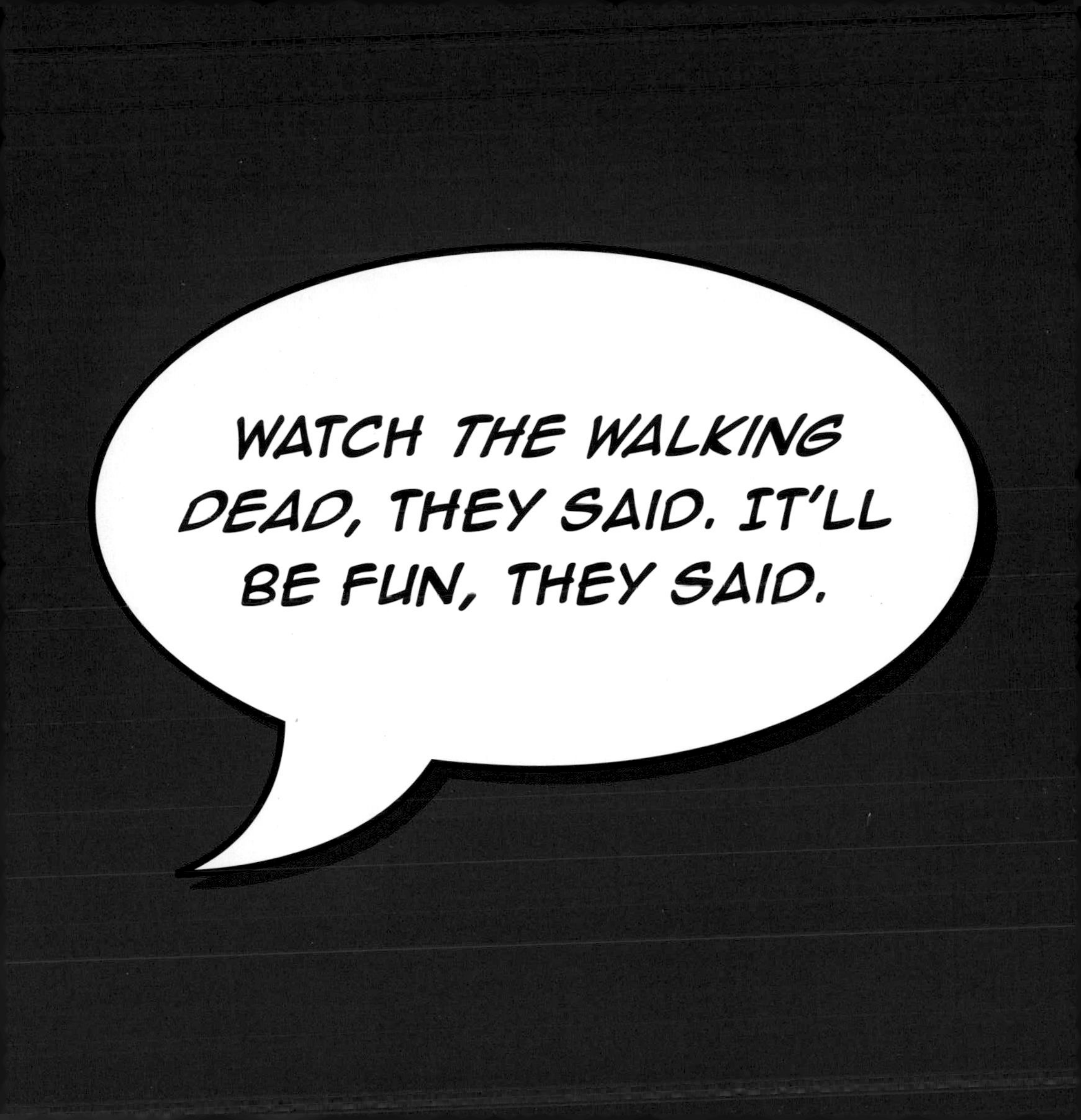
WATCH THE WALKING DEAD, THEY SAID. IT'LL BE FUN, THEY SAID.

IF I JUST STRETCH A *LITTLE* MORE, I CAN REACH THE REMOTE WITHOUT MOVING!

LET ME SEE: ADD THE 10 AND THE 4, MULTIPLY BY 50, AND . . . OH, THIS IS HARD!

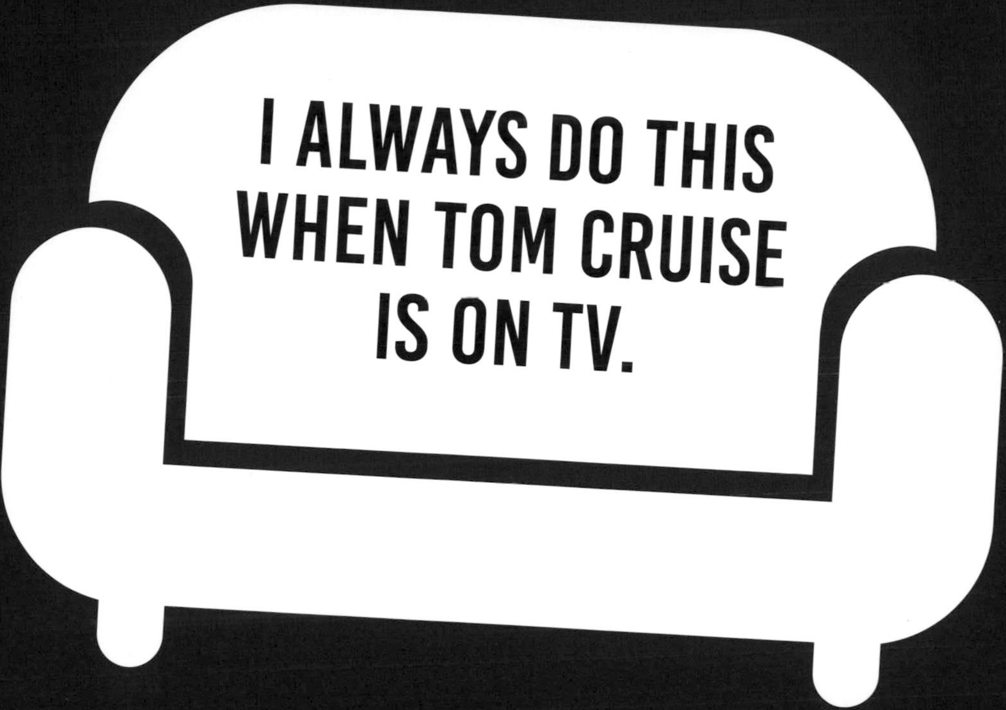
I ALWAYS DO THIS
WHEN TOM CRUISE
IS ON TV.

SOMETIMES A GOOD DOCUMENTARY CAN REALLY MAKE YOU THINK . . . .

IT'S GONNA BE THIS WEEK,
IT'S GONNA BE ME THIS WEEK,
COME ON, LUCKY NUMBERS . . .

WHY DO I WATCH THIS EVERY YEAR?

RAWR! MOVE OVER, GODZILLA!

IT'S NOT CHEATING, MABEL. I JUST LIKE TO BE ABLE TO CHECK MY ANSWERS DURING THE COUNTDOWN.

A LIKELY STORY . . .

IF I HAVE TO WATCH ONE MORE DANCING DOG GETTING THROUGH TO THE FINALS . . .

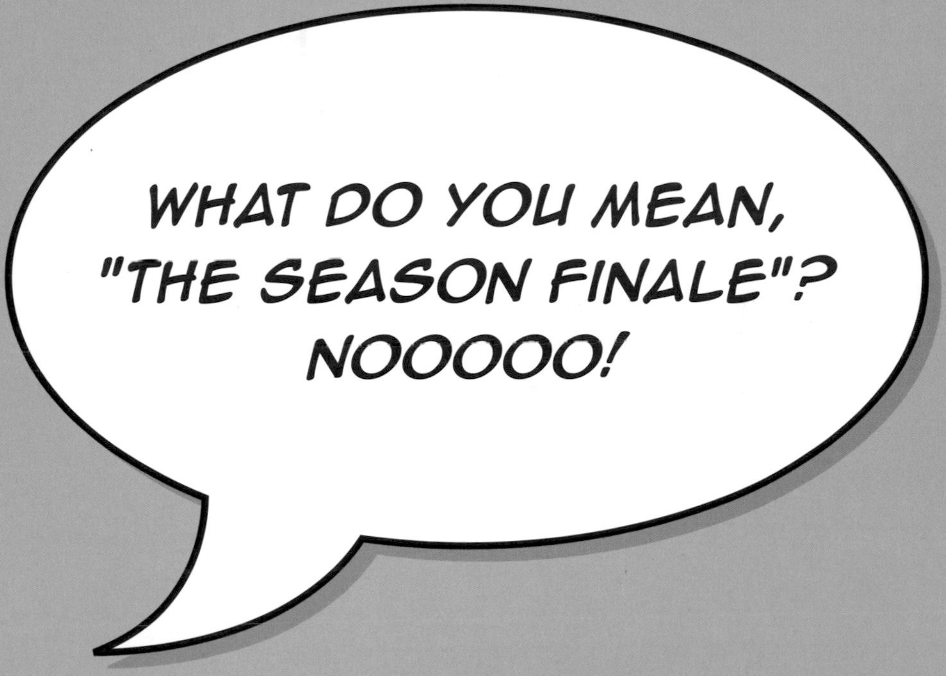
WHAT DO YOU MEAN, "THE SEASON FINALE"? NOOOOO!

YES, I'M ON A DIET, BUT I CAN WATCH *DINERS, DRIVE-INS, AND DIVES* ALL DAY IF I WANT TO.

HA! WHO'D EVER WANT
TO GO OUT WITH SOMEONE
WITH A FACE AS FUNNY
AS THAT?

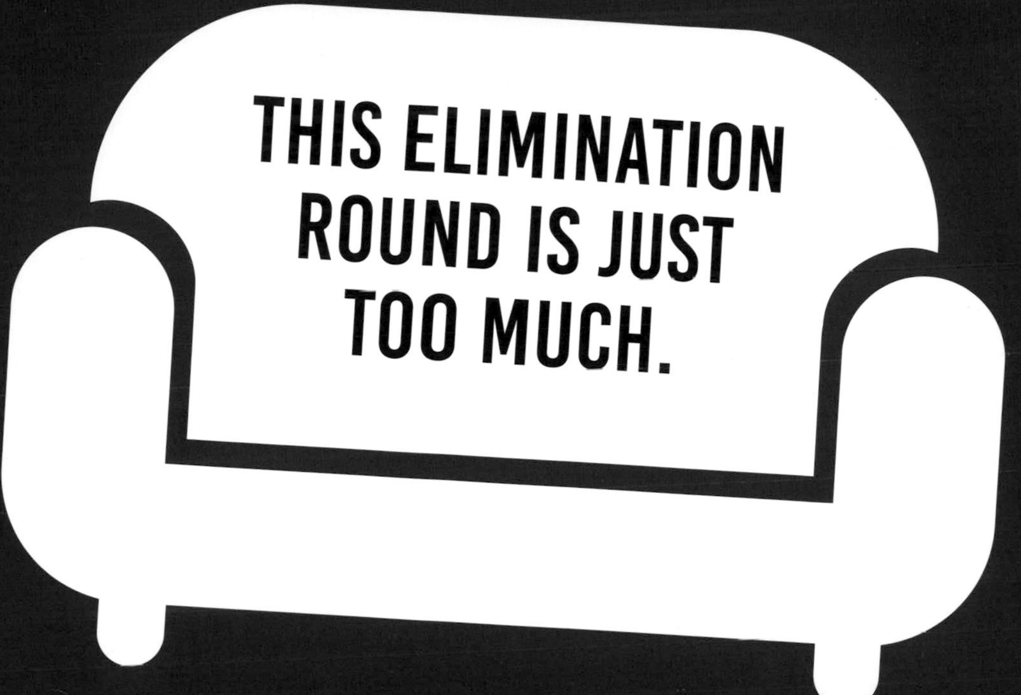
THIS ELIMINATION
ROUND IS JUST
TOO MUCH.

LOOK, I NEED THE WHOLE SOFA OR I CAN'T STRETCH OUT PROPERLY. YOU'VE GOT A PERFECTLY NICE BLANKET ON THE FLOOR, DON'T YOU?

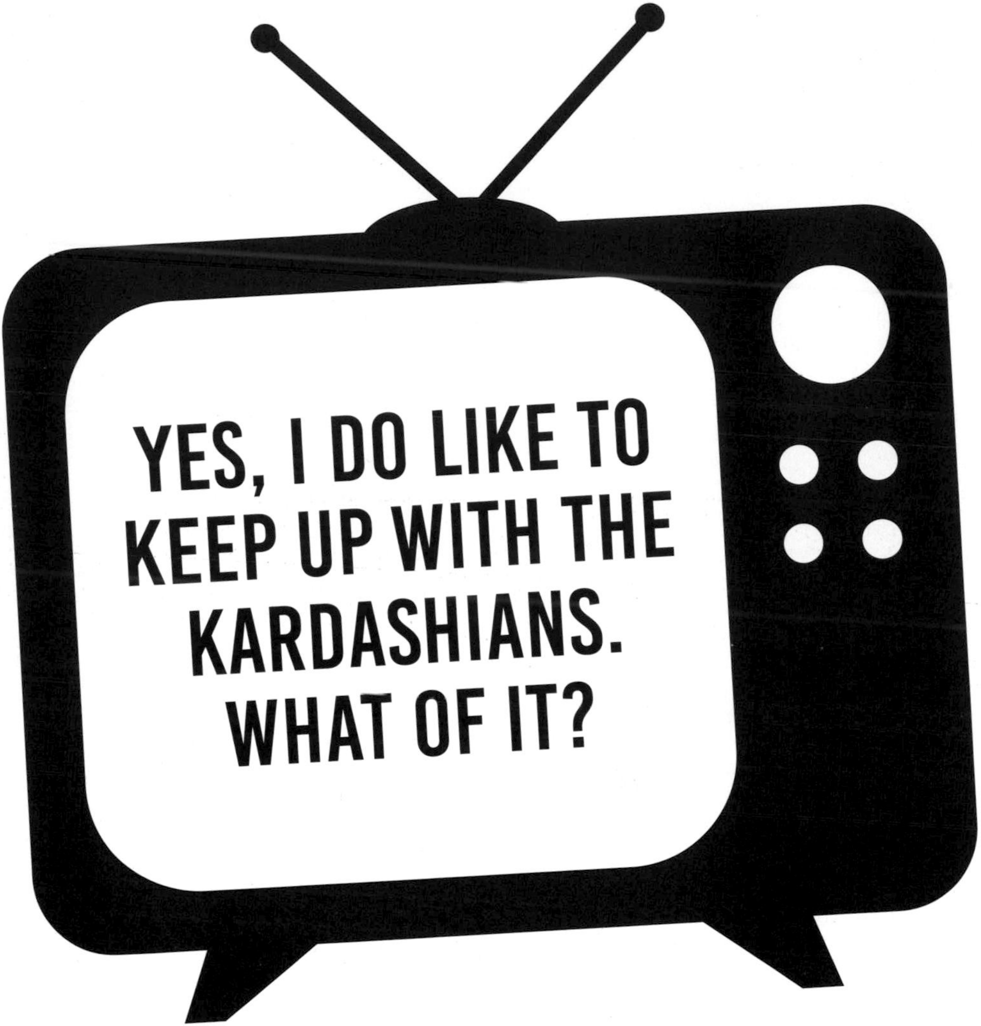
YES, I DO LIKE TO
KEEP UP WITH THE
KARDASHIANS.
WHAT OF IT?

WELL, I COULD GO OUTSIDE . . . OR I COULD WATCH ANOTHER EPISODE OF HOMELAND.

WE'RE THINKING OF APPLYING FOR *MARRIAGE BOOT CAMP*, BUT BRIAN NEEDS SOME PERSUADING. DON'T YOU, BRIAN?

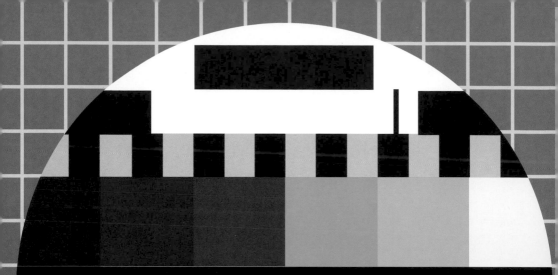

AND NOW ANOTHER TEN MINUTES OF COMMERCIALS.

SORRY, I KNOW WE AGREED IT'S YOUR DATE NIGHT TONIGHT, BUT I JUST LOVE FRIENDS. I'M NOT IN THE WAY, AM I?

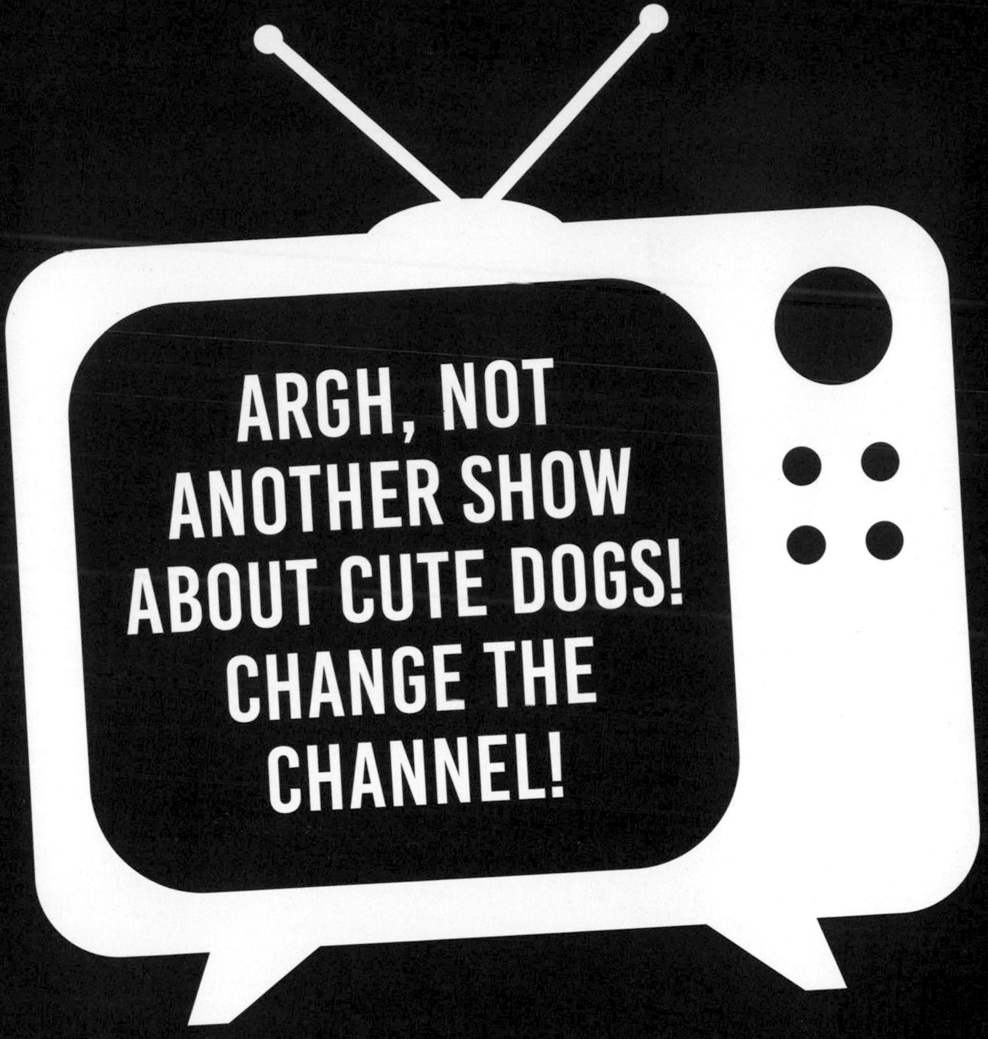
ARGH, NOT
ANOTHER SHOW
ABOUT CUTE DOGS!
CHANGE THE
CHANNEL!

WHAT DO YOU MEAN GREY'S ANATOMY HAS BEEN POSTPONED FOR A WEEK DUE TO FOOTBALL?

STUCK BETWEEN THESE CUSHIONS?
OH NO, DEFINITELY NOT. I COULD
LEAVE IF I WANTED TO.

(PLEASE HELP ME.)

NOW, ARE YOU SURE YOU DON'T WANT TO THINK TWICE ABOUT CHANGING THE CHANNEL? IT WOULD BE SUCH A SHAME IF THIS LEATHER SOFA GOT . . . SCRATCHED . . .

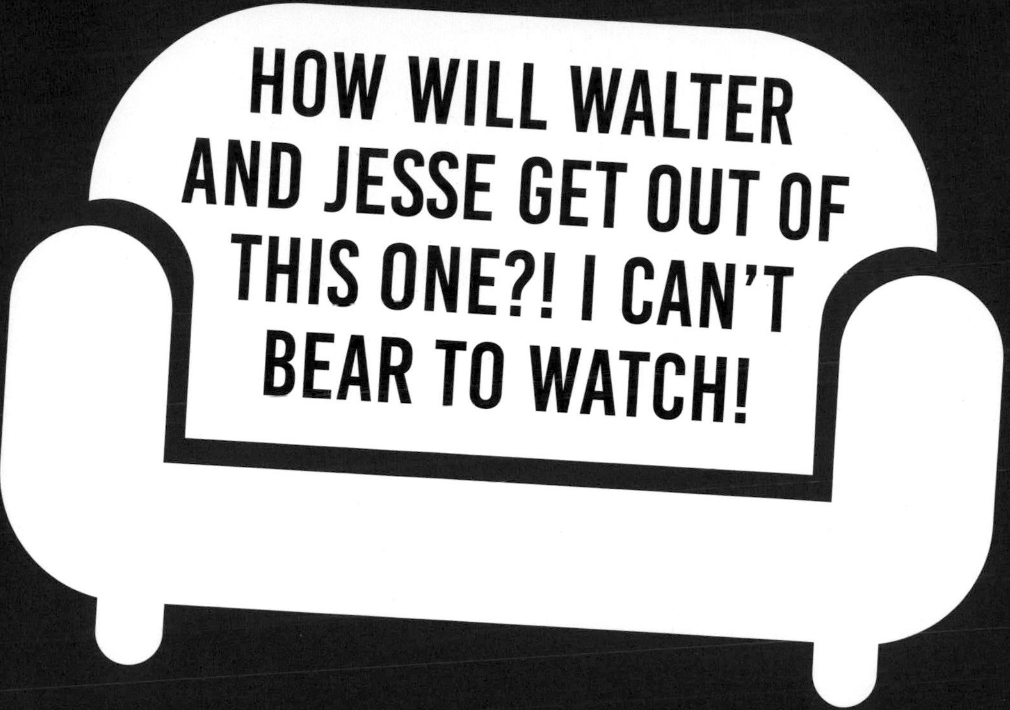
HOW WILL WALTER AND JESSE GET OUT OF THIS ONE?! I CAN'T BEAR TO WATCH!

IF ONLY OUR CHAIR SWIVELED LIKE THOSE ONES, WE WOULDN'T HAVE TO WATCH THIS TRAIN WRECK.

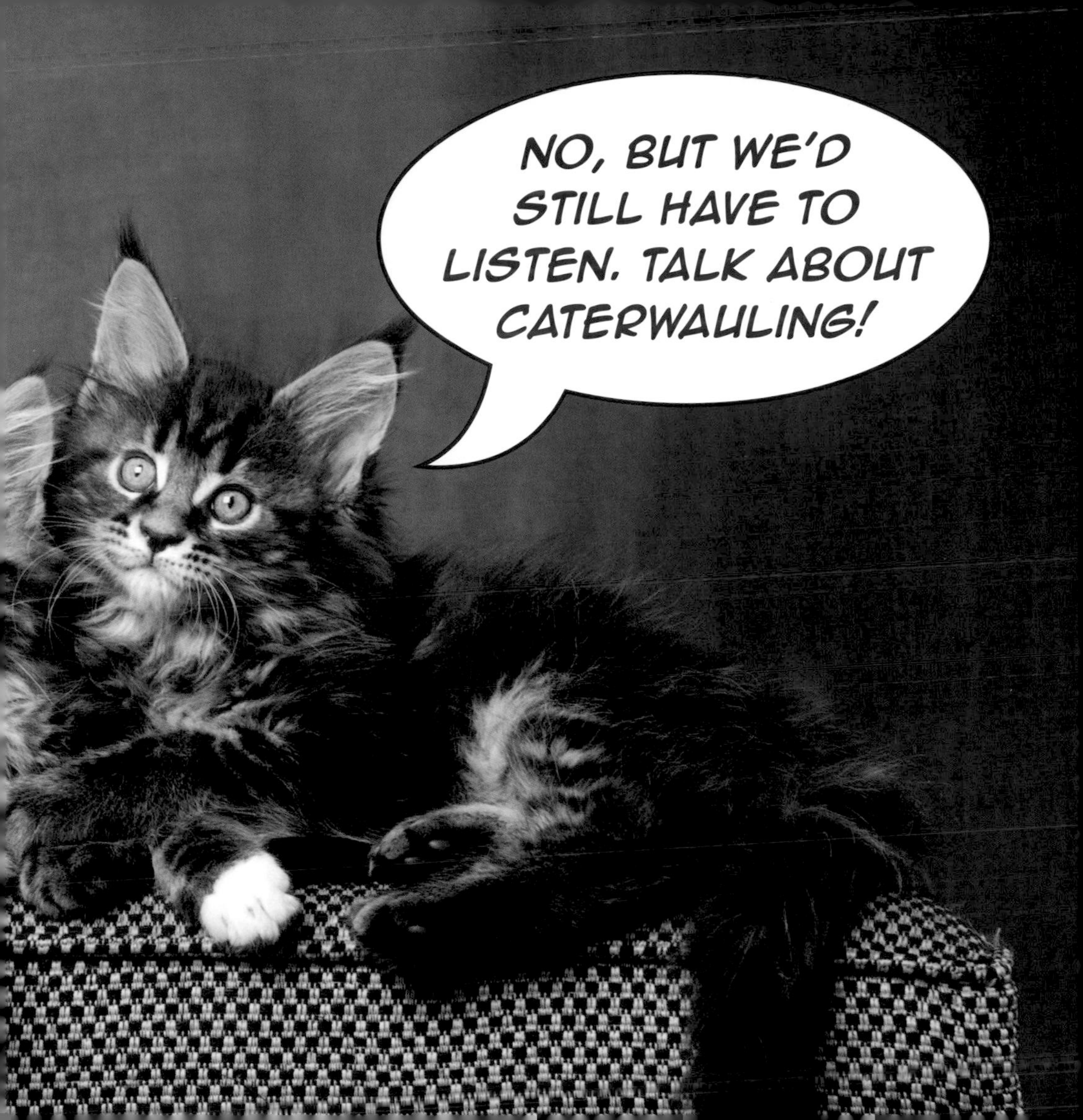
NO, BUT WE'D STILL HAVE TO LISTEN. TALK ABOUT CATERWAULING!

I'M NOT VERY GOOD AT WATCHING SCARY MOVIES . . . CAN YOU HOLD MY PAW?

EXCUSE ME, NOBODY WARNED ME THERE WERE GOING TO BE DOGS IN THIS WESTMINSTER NONSENSE. TIME TO TURN OVER, I THINK!

I WON'T SLEEP A WINK TONIGHT!
I SHOULD NEVER HAVE STAYED UP
FOR *AMERICAN HORROR STORY*.

**AND, BOOM! HOW'S THIS FOR A POSE? I COULD DO BETTER THAN THOSE GIRLS ON *AMERICA'S NEXT TOP MODEL* ANY DAY.**

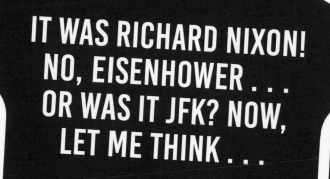

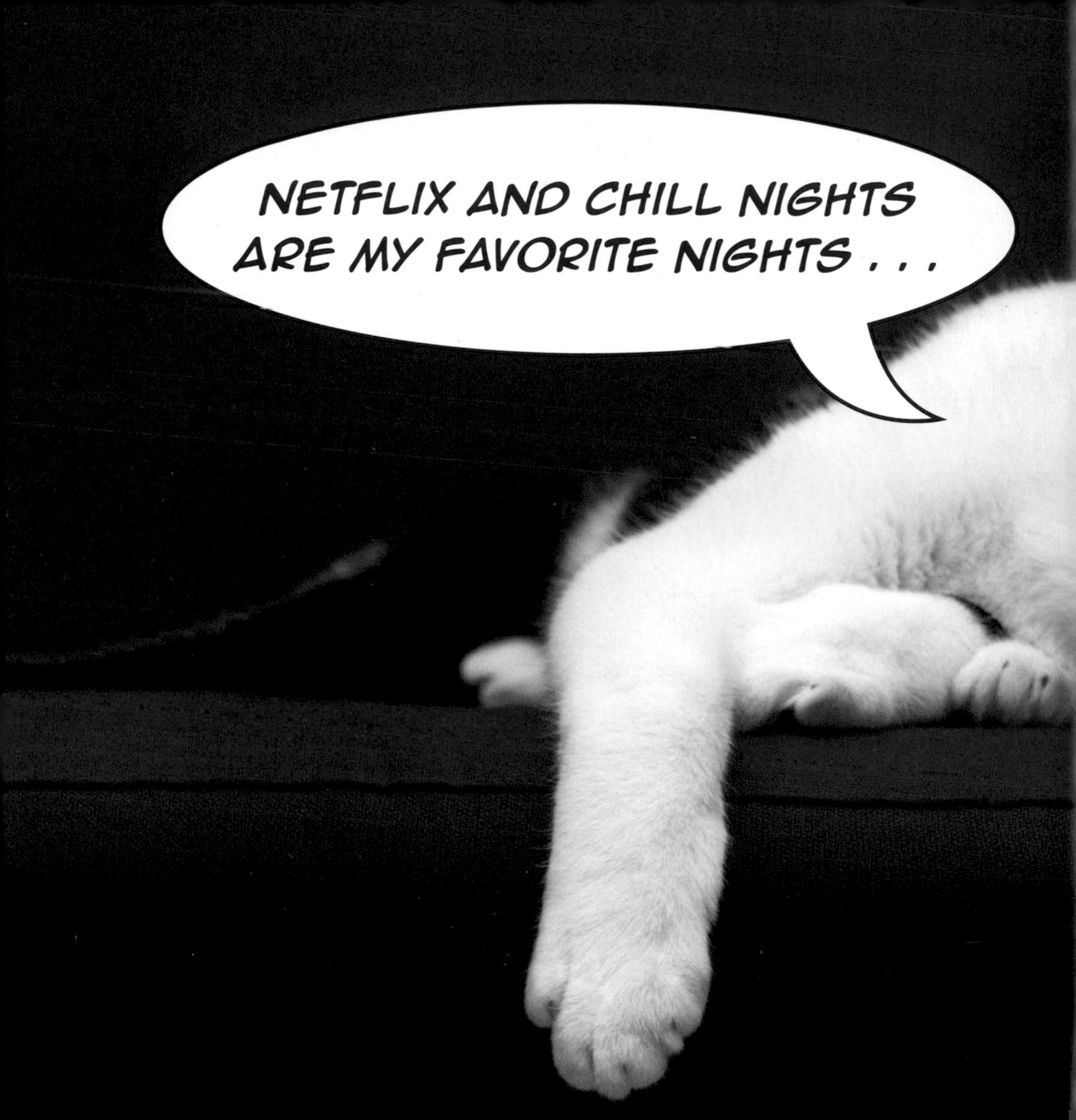
NETFLIX AND CHILL NIGHTS ARE MY FAVORITE NIGHTS . . .

I HAVE TO ADMIT, THAT FRIED CHICKEN DOES LOOK PAW-LICKIN' GOOD . . .

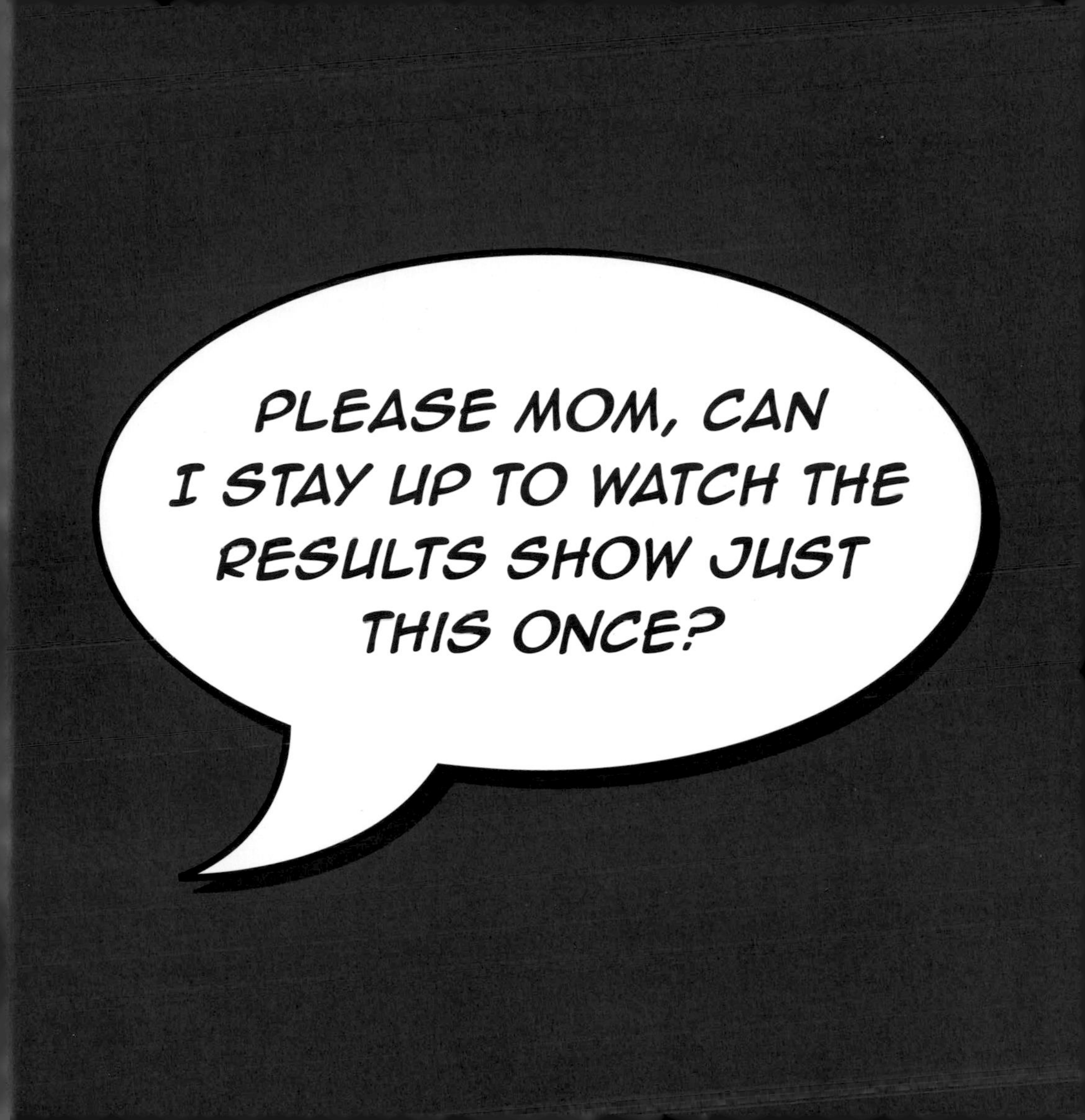
PLEASE MOM, CAN I STAY UP TO WATCH THE RESULTS SHOW JUST THIS ONCE?

I DON'T KNOW WHY YOU'RE LAUGHING—ISN'T THIS HOW ALL CATS WATCH TV?

**COUNTRIES THAT BORDER TURKEY? RIGHT . . . OOH . . . I KNOW THIS ONE . . . I'M SURE I CAN GET A POINTLESS ANSWER THIS TIME!**

TWENTY-FOUR-
HOUR TV HASN'T
AFFECTED US AT ALL,
HAS IT, DARLING?
DARLING . . . ?

# PHOTO CREDITS

# GAME OF BONES

CHARLIE ELLIS

**WHAT YOUR DOG REALLY THINKS WHILE YOU WATCH TV**

# ALSO AVAILABLE